The Art of Manifestation
Astro-Moon Journal
2021

from the I Choose Love Series.
The Pathway of the Spiritual Warrior.

The Art of Manifestation

Astro-Moon Journal 2021

This Journal Belongs to

....

The Art of Manifestation Astro-Moon Journal 2021
From the I Choose Love Series
The Pathway of the Spiritual Warrior

The Art of Manifestation Astro-Moon Journal
First Published 2019 A-Z of Emotional Health Ltd.
©2019 Jenny Florence/Burgess The A-Z of Emotional Health Ltd.
Published by the A-Z of Emotional Health Ltd.

The Art of Manifestation
Astro-Moon Journal

Welcome to 2021

Contents

My dear friends, what extraordinary times we are living in.
Having immersed myself in the astro-energy of the coming year it is clear that whilst 2021 brings a different energetic focus or flavor to that of 2020, it is equally powerful and continues to reinforce the need for change.

If 2020 was a year in which the Universe stopped us in our tracks and asked us to listen and to review, then the astrology of 2021 requests that we take this a step further and initiate and implement the changes needed to forge new ways of living that will create a genuinely sustainable future that honors and respects all of life that surrounds us on this beautiful planet.

My deepest respect goes out to you all, for in using books and resources like this, you make a personal choice to walk a conscious path in alignment with the natural energy of the greater universal consciousness, the stuff of the stars and the very substance of who we are.

Namaste

The Art of Manifestation

The art of manifestation involves not only imagining and dreaming of the kind of life that we wish to have, we must also take actions that enable our dreams to find form. Our state of mind, our attitudes and perceptions, and the way that we feel, our emotions, all have an impact on our ability to fully immerse ourselves in this creative process.

It seems to me that manifestation has its own cyclical and natural pattern of evolution.

- We listen to our desires, and we allow ourselves to dream.
- We imagine possibilities and we honor their potential.
- We evaluate and decide what steps we must take to initiate these possibilities into form.
- Remaining open to ongoing evaluation, we commit to a pathway forward.
- We persevere in our doing, trusting that any diversions and interruptions are sent to us to bring greater meaning, clarity, and direction.
- When needed, whether in our external actions or deep within our own psyche, we identify any ongoing work that we need to do to keep the energy flowing.
- We continue our ongoing pathway of evolution and co-creativity, and we trust that we will always be shown the next steps.
- Listening to the wisdom and guidance of the universe, when needed we course correct.
- Trusting that the universe knows of our fullest potential and holds a higher vision for us that is greater than we ourselves could possibly imagine, we understand that we will be given what we need, although not always necessarily what we want.
- Our pathway emerges and our dreams begin to take form.

How to Use this Journal

This journal can be used independently in its own right or used alongside the Art of Manifestation Diary. Both will assist you in understanding how best to align with and use, the incoming astro-energy in support of your own process of conscious manifestation.

Astrological information is not designed to tell us what to do, it does however offer us an indication of the kind of energetic influences at any given time, and as such acts as an invaluable road map supporting our ability to navigate our lives form a position of conscious, mindful choice.

The primary focus of The Art of Manifestation Diary is to build and strengthen your personal relationship with the daily positioning of the Moon. As well as highlighting key phases of the Moon, with some further information about the incoming energy and potential influences of some of the other major collaborations and planetary connections, you will also find additional monthly guidance from both Oracle Cards and Runes to assist in navigating the incoming energy with full awareness.

The Art of Manifestation Journal offers a more in-depth account of the monthly astrological influences, with specific details as to how best to navigate the incoming energy. There is also additional information about working with the dynamics of the New Moon and the Full Moon to add energetic weight to your personal process of manifestation.

The Journal is divided into twelve monthly sections with a selection of both lined and clear pages for journaling. Each section begins with a run down of the astrological collaborations for the coming month plus specific information on how best to utilize the New Moon energy to enhance the setting of wishes and intentions, and the Full Moon energy to bring spiritual illumination and heightened awareness.

Each month, the journal also draws on the natural properties of a particular stone or crystal that aligns with the overall astrological dynamic of the month, with information about how these natural healers of the Earth can aid and support us, particularly during times of accelerated growth and transition.

In both the journal and the diary, you will find a section at the beginning with information about the different phases of the Moon, including the impact of both solar and lunar eclipses, plus a description of the way that the lunar energy is affected and channeled as the Moon travels through each sign of the zodiac. I have also explained the potential impact of the influences of the various planets in retrograde and listed the dates that these events occur.

To complete our understanding of how best to attune ourselves with the natural rhythms and cycles of the turning of the seasons, I have also shared some thoughts about the way in which we can navigate the shifts in energy that take place at the solstices and the equinoxes, so we can fully appreciate and understand the relevance of these pivotal moments of natural transition in the context of our manifestations.

The Power of Collective Prayer

From an astrological perspective, during 2021 we can expect to see three peak periods of particularly powerful energetic intensity.

To ensure that we center ourselves in the higher vibration of this energetic, please join me for one minute of silent prayer at 7pm each day during these periods.

The dates which take place in February, June and December are noted throughout the journal. I will also be posting reminders on all of the AZEmotionalHealth Social Media Channels.

Do please spread the word.

The Phases of the Moon

The New Moon.

The new moon is traditionally associated with the setting of wishes and intentions and so the energy at this time naturally invites us to meditate into a space of possibility. If you are a daily meditator, you may already find that for the two days before and the two days after the new moon, your mind may be inclined to wander during your meditations.

If this is the case you may find it helpful to have a pen and paper close by, or use the journaling pages in this diary to make a note of any ideas that come to you during your meditation practice. Personally, during this phase of the moon, I find myself naturally drawn to walking meditations.

Consciously make the effort to spend time outdoors and immerse yourself in nature and whatever your preferred way of finding stillness, calm your mind, and enter your own dreamtime. Let your mind wander into the depths of the new moon energy and give yourself permission to dream big!

The Crescent Moon.

In the phase of the crescent moon the seeds that emerged at the new moon will begin to whisper to you, calling to be heard. How we respond to this inner calling will have a direct influence on our ability to be proactive in our developing process of manifestation.

Take your yearnings and your desires seriously and notice any thinking patterns that may be holding you back or limiting your perspectives. In the process of manifestation, we are both doers and deciders and so the extent of our external manifestations will always be a reflection of our ability to embrace our inner growth. At this time, any resistance to change can be identified, paving the way for this month's cycle of inner growth.

The crescent moon invites us to identify any resistances within us, any patterns of thinking or self-sabotaging attitudes and behaviors that may limit us from stepping into the fullest potential of our dreams. Our very recognition of these patterns will automatically diminish their power as well as opening up opportunities and avenues of potential healing and resolution.

The First Quarter Moon.

The first quarter moon is sometimes thought of as a time when hurdles and obstacles that need to be overcome, will push forwards and enter into our awareness. Personally, I have found that the energy of the first quarter moon affects me in a far more vibrant and positive way.

During this phase of the moon, having identified any inner blocks to progress, during the crescent moon, the seeds of ideas that were planted at the new moon, push themselves forwards in abundance, and I find myself flooded with thoughts of what I will need to do to nurture the possibilities of the new moon, to enable them to begin to take shape and manifest into real form.

I look carefully at the scope of my ideas and begin to focus on those which are most important for me to initiate at this moment in time. The combination of the seeds of the new moon and the learning discovered at the crescent moon, enables me to prioritize and to formulate my actions for the coming month.

The Gibbous Moon.

In the time of the gibbous moon energy is building, passions are high, and dreams are calling to be made real. Ideas begin to take shape, and the pathway forward gains clarity. Taking time to hold my intentions and my vision for the future in mind, I ground myself in the present moment, and I request guidance in knowing which steps to take in the here and now, before turning my decisions into acts of doing.

Take time to celebrate the joy to be found in the excitement of anticipation, whilst remaining present and grounded. Hold your vision but treasure the here and now moments of your journey and be available to receive guidance. Stay on track, but simultaneously be open to any course corrections that you are guided towards.

The Full Moon.

The power and energy of the full moon is extraordinary. For anyone who works with healing stones and crystals, be sure to place them outside overnight to recharge in the eliminating power of the full moon. Their energy of release and repair will be revitalized for any healing work over the coming month.

The full brightness of this powerful and highly charged energy brings a space of authenticity where all is revealed and illuminated, and so the full moon is often a time when we experience heightened and intense emotions.

Be kind to yourself and others. Notice and listen, particularly to any situations that are not okay. Things that are usually tolerated or brushed under the carpet will surface and request your attention. So, if you find yourself experiencing any challenging emotions please take them seriously.

The energy of this phase of the moon brings a wonderful opportunity to notice, to listen, to reflect, and then to release and let go, clearing the way to move forwards.

In the process of manifestation, if we find ourselves unable to move forwards or feel stuck in some way, it is often some aspect of our past that is still lingering, blocking us from believing in ourselves or believing in others or finding trust in the possibility of a different future. Anyone who has ever experienced trauma or abuse will tell you that whilst the physical scars will heal, it is the emotional ones that remain.

The full moon illuminates our emotions highlighting exactly what is working for us... as well as anything that is not!

Learn to differentiate between emotions that connect to past experiences, as opposed to emotions that are part of your immediate response system helping you to navigate your life in the here and now. There is a difference!

Our emotions contain and generate energy. Understanding this difference between past and present emotional influences allows you to identify anything that you need to release from the past, empowering you to channel any highly charged emotional energy into positive action.

If you find yourself struggling with challenging emotional states, you may find 'Mindfulness Meets Emotional Awareness - 7 steps to learn the language of your emotions' a useful read. This book explains exactly how and why our most challenging emotions serve us and will teach you how to transform and channel any highly charged emotions into actions that support your pathway rather than hinder it.

The Disseminating Moon.

As the energy of the full moon diminishes, emotions are released, and forgiveness is discovered. This phase of the moon brings opportunity to step into a position of authentic empowerment. Within this energetic space of emergence, we hold awareness of ourselves, of others and in alignment with the collective soul of humanity, the disseminating Moon invites us to be all that we can be.

This is a time to acknowledge and validate the extraordinariness of who you are, and of everything, both good and bad, that has led you to the place that you stand today and contributed to the person that you are.

Be steady in your actions and in your doings. Stand in your power and be your true self with joy, gratitude, and humility. Let the energy of the disseminating moon filter into every cell of your body, affirming your dedication to your pathway.

The Last Quarter Moon.

The energy of the last quarter moon invites us to walk our talk. If the full moon energy gives us an opportunity to upgrade our system, letting go of anything that no longer serves us, then the last quarter moon is a time that invites us to integrate our learning and to follow it through in all that we do and in all that we are.

The energy of this moon brings us the opportunity to make sure that our plans, actions and decisions are congruent with all that we wish to be and all that we wish to see in the world.

Stand firm and pay attention to the details of your world and notice if any adjustments need to be made. From a spiritual perspective, do you need to cross any T's or dot any I's to ensure that in all areas of your life, you are living in congruence with your truest values and deepest desires. Within the unique circumstances of your own process of co-creativity are you 'being' everything that you wish to attract for yourself.

For example, how positive are your thoughts? Does your inner critic offer constructive feedback or harsh criticism? Are you kinder to others than to yourself? ... or is it the other way around?

Centre yourself in compassion, kindness, and above all... in love.

The Balsamic Moon.

The balsamic Moon asks you to trust. Hold your vision, and yet simultaneously let go of any attachment to specific outcomes. This is a time of preparation and nurture, a time to fertilize the ground in anticipation of the coming new moon and of any new seeds that you may wish to sow.

Keep your energy clean and be particularly aware of your personal energetic resonance. Self-responsibility can be understood to mean 'our ability to be responsive to ourselves'. From an energetic perspective, be sure to cleanse yourself of anything that clings and that may no longer be serving you. Centre yourself in the knowledge that as this monthly lunar phase comes to its completion, you can engage in preparing the ground for your own deliverance, making space within for the emergence of a new cycle of opportunity.

Validate, acknowledge, and cherish all that you have achieved during this last phase of manifestation, and in your reflections, remember that there is no wrong way. Anything that appears to have been a wrong turn or a mistake will have led you to exactly the place that you need to be, right now, bringing you the awareness that you needed to take fresh new steps as we approach the coming energy of the next new moon.

The Moon in the Zodiac Signs

Moon in Aries.

At this emotionally powerful time, use the energy to be assertive and to initiate your ideas. Say how it is and take action.

Moon in Taurus.

Grounded, sensual and earthy, use this energy to attune yourself with the natural rhythms of nature. A great time for walking meditations.

Moon in Gemini.

A time of communication, reaching out and connecting with others, use this energy for networking and socializing.

Moon in Cancer.

A wonderful time to be at home, share food and be in the company of family and close friends. Use this energy to nourish your soul, spending time with those you love.

Moon in Leo.

Sing, laugh, express yourself and find your voice. Use this energy to feel alive and embrace the joy of self-discovery and self-expression. We are never too old to play!

Moon in Virgo.

This energy supports us in attending to any work that requires dedication, structure, order and precision. Approach your tasks with willingness and a desire to serve.

Moon in Libra.

The energy of this moon calls us to seek harmony and to find balance. This is a time to share and to discover ourselves through our relationships and the company of others.

Moon in Scorpio.

A time to journey inwards, this energy connects us to the depths of our unconscious and can bring deep emotions to the surface. Be sure to listen to yourself and take your yearnings seriously.

Moon in Sagittarius.

The energy of this moon invites us to vision in an optimistic future, full of hope and possibility. A great time to expand our horizons and dream big!

Moon in Capricorn.

The energy of this moon invites us to take pragmatic, practical actions to manifest our ideas into form. Get building and embrace the joy of doing.

Moon in Aquarius.

A time to collaborate, share ideas and work together. The energy of this moon invites you to align your individual contribution with a higher vision of greater purpose that will also serve the collective Soul of humanity.

Moon in Pisces.

A time to dream and a time to heal. Open yourself to divine inspiration and allow yourself to be guided. The energy of this moon brings illumination, fuelling imagination and creativity.

Solar and Lunar Eclipses

During eclipse season, the already intense energy of both the new and full moons are intensified. An eclipse in your sign, will always be a significant trigger point or turning point in your own personal process of evolution and can often herald random events that create sudden and unexpected changes.

On your personal journey of manifestation, understanding this heightened and intensified energy can be incredibly helpful in knowing, when to reflect and set your intentions, and when to take action to move something forwards, particularly if you intend to make or initiate significant changes in any aspect of your life.

Eclipses are also associated with our Karmic journey, creating an energetic rift that overrides our usual perception and connection to time. The energy of the eclipses is said to open an energetic portal that assists us in connecting with our purpose and calling in this present lifetime.

Symbolized in the tarot pack by the cards of Death and the Tower, the energy of both the solar and lunar eclipses are associated with transformation, either internally or in the circumstances of our external lives, and often involves both endings and new beginnings.

When we learn to work with the influence of the eclipses, rather than trying to control events, we consciously make time to allow the energy of a greater universal consciousness to flow through us, bringing us the guidance that we need to support the evolution of our Soul within our human experience.

Solar Eclipse.

A solar eclipse is when the moon sits in between the sun and the earth, with the moon covering the sun. This will always occur at a new moon. The energy associated with this time is the same as a new moon, but intensified, like a new moon on steroids!

This is the perfect time to get still and to meditate into a space of personal dreamtime and allow your ideas to flow.

The energy of the solar eclipse can bring an extraordinary surge of creative possibilities, although these may not always arrive in the shape or form that we expect. If you are already involved in setting intentions, but then find that something happens to suddenly create a shift in your direction, trust that this unexpected change is important to your personal growth and evolution, and connected to the calling of your soul.

In matters of manifestation, the universe will always have the upper hand and tends to bring us what we need... although not always what we want!

When we can allow ourselves to trust that even in moments of upheaval and disruption we are being gifted with an opportunity, we open ourselves to receive the fullest potential and the greatest learning to be found in every situation.

Lunar Eclipse.

A lunar eclipse is when the earth sits between the moon and the sun, and this will always occur at a full moon. Full moons are associated with heightened emotions and during a lunar eclipse, emotions can run high, like a full moon on steroids!

If we think of the moon as our Feminine Guardian who circles our planet, gathering the energy of the sun and redistributing it to the earth in various measures, at the time of a Lunar Eclipse, the energy of the moon is like a fully charged battery, highly charged and ready to ignite change.

In the full illumination of the moon at her most powerful, all is revealed. Anything and everything that is running smoothly and working in service of a balanced and authentic life will be apparent to us, confirming that we are walking the right path. Likewise, anything and everything that is not working for us or no longer serves us, both internally and externally, will also be brought into the light, calling to be addressed, changed, and if necessary, released.

As long as something remains hidden or unconscious, we are helpless to address the issue and to take actions of resolution, however, when we identify a problem, the very fact that we can see the issue clearly creates an opportunity to seek solutions and find ways forward. On our personal journey of manifestation, the energy of a lunar eclipse increases our connections with any emotional residue from the past that may be clinging and coloring our perspectives inappropriately, creating an amazing opportunity for cleansing and release, clearing the way for resolution and healing. This is a powerful time to embrace forgiveness, of both ourselves and others.

Lunar eclipses are often associated with external changes that are a mirror or a reflection of our internal growth and learning. Whatever is taking place around you, if something in your life appears to be needing to change or to leave, let go gracefully and know that it is timely to the evolution of your soul.

If you are naturally a highly empathic person and particularly sensitive to the feelings of others, at the time of a lunar eclipse you may find yourself highly absorbent to the emotional states of the people around you. Be sure to cleanse and do a daily release ceremony to let go of anything that doesn't belong to you before meditating into your own space of illumination.

- 26 May – 11.19 GMT - Full Moon Lunar Eclipse 5°29' Sagittarius
- 10 June – 10.43 GMT - New Moon Solar Eclipse 19°42' Gemini
- 19 November – 09.04 GMT - Full Moon Lunar Eclipse 27°17' Taurus
- 04 December – 07.34 GMT New Moon Solar Eclipse 12°16' Sagittarius

The Planets in Retrograde 2021

The Inner Planets, Mercury and Venus.

Mercury in Retrograde.

- 30th January 26° Aquarius – 21st February 11° Aquarius
- 29th May 24° Gemini – 22nd June 16° Gemini
- 27th September 25° Libra – 18th October 10° Libra

The energy of Mercury in retrograde is often associated with obstructions and delays, and in our target and goal orientated culture, we understandably tend to experience this period through a negative lens. Mercury retrograde periods seem to cause us no end of disruption, our plans go astray, we experience roadblocks and diversions, and there are often difficulties with our IT and communication systems.

However, if we step away from this viewpoint and consider that all aspects of planetary influences can support us and bring us valuable and necessary gifts, this shift in our perspective enables us to stand back and work with the incoming energy.

If there is a diversion, then the universe may be giving you a sign, perhaps you are meant to take an alternative route where you will discover something that was absolutely essential to your personal growth and evolution.

If something from your past raises its head during a Mercury retrograde period, then your attention is required. This is an invitation for you to acknowledge this issue and take time to embark on the necessary steps to lay it to rest.

There will always be times in our lives when the energy is with us to set targets and remain fixed on our course, to plough forwards and to push and to strive, however, given that the energy of Mercury represents our capacity to develop and integrate wisdom on our souls' journey within the human experience, when the Winged Messenger of the Gods temporarily stands still in the heavens and appears to travel backwards, this energy calls us back and asks us to slow down, to take our time and to be alert to any signals and signs that the universe is trying to show us.

Venus in Retrograde.

- **19ᵗʰ December 26° Capricorn – 29ᵗʰ January 2022 11° Capricorn**

Are you in balance? Do you allow yourself to receive as much as you give and vice versa? Are you actively involved in your own self-care? Do you pause to celebrate your achievements along the way, and do you give yourself an appropriate amount of time out to relax?

Self-care is not an act of selfishness; it is an act of consciousness.

When Venus moves into retrograde the energy of the feminine invites you to listen to your heart, to override the demands of a busy mind and be centered in your truest values, including and especially your own self-care.

Venus is in retrograde is a wonderful time to reflect and to realign and rebalance all areas of your life. This revitalizing influence of this phase will keep your energy clean and flowing and ensure that your energetic resonance is congruent with all that you wish to manifest into the world. As such, Venus in retrograde plays an essential role in our ability to manifest our truest desires.

During periods of transition, if you have ever found yourself questioning what your true calling might be, when Venus is in retrograde, ask for guidance and be open to receive.

If during this time you find yourself called to stand up for your values, the female warrior energy of Venus will support you in connecting with the lioness within. In the name of kindness, compassion and peace, her retrograde energy will encourage you to find your authentic voice, speak the truth, and stand firm in your boundaries.

The Transpersonal Planets, Jupiter and Saturn.

Jupiter in Retrograde.

- **20ᵗʰ June 02° Pisces – 18ᵗʰ October 22° Aquarius**

A time of powerful personal growth, Jupiter in retrograde invites us on an inward quest of self-discovery seeking the knowledge and illumination that will enable us to stand in our own truth and walk our talk.

Jupiter is known as the planet of good luck and good fortune and from the perspective of manifestation, during the retrograde period we can expect to have experiences that cause us to look within and seek answers of a Spiritual nature.

The Jupiter retrograde energy helps us to forge our true values and to attune with our greater purpose and as such, during this period, windows of opportunity may open that illuminate issues from the past, including past lives, presenting us with the opportunity to find resolution and align with our true calling at this present moment of our journey.

Any internal growth and changes made during this time will then in turn, manifest outwardly and Jupiter returns to a forward flow of expansion.

Saturn in Retrograde.

- **23rd May 13° Aquarius – 11th October 06° Aquarius**

When the planet Saturn, known as Father Time and the planet of Karma, moves into retrograde, any aspects of our lives that need restructuring and reorganizing will come to a head.

We will be shown exactly what is working in our lives, alongside any aspects of our world that are not!

The lessons of Saturn can feel quite harsh as the energy calls us to account, speaking in the name of "Tough Love", however, the Saturn retrograde energy is not without reward!

The more open we are to embracing the natural evolutionary process of "weeding and pruning", letting go gracefully of anything that no longer serves us or has outlived its purpose, whether these are physical aspects of our lives or indeed any internal attitudes and beliefs, then the more smoothly these periods of profound transition will emerge.

The words "emergence" and "emergency" both come from the same source.

Saturn retrograde energy reminds us that change is both necessary and natural and that we live in a continual space of learning, not only from those wonderful experiences that fill us with joy, but also from the experiences that do not feel good and do not resonate with us.

From the perspective of manifestation a valuable part of our ability to become consciously and actively co-creative in our lives is to be able to recognize and listen to all of our experiences, both good and bad, and to use the more challenging ones as a source of inspiration and guidance.

Rather than dwell on the negative, we can use the information from that experience to define our desires with greater clarity. This in turn opens us to receive the guidance and direction that we need to manifest those desires that resonate with us at a core level of Soul.

The Outer Planets, Uranus, Neptune and Pluto.

The energy of the outer planets is slow moving which means that their influence is deep and penetrating creating significant growth stages with long term implications. In our individual natal charts, the positioning of these planets will not only have personal implications but will also be an indicator of generational traits.

Uranus in Retrograde.

- 15th August 2020 10° Taurus – 14th January 06° Taurus
- 20th August 14° Taurus – 18th January 2022 10° Taurus

Uranus is known as the Great Awakener and the bringer of sudden changes. I always see his energy as a Lightening Spirit bringing us those thunderbolt moments where we know in no uncertain terms that something needs to change. The energy might arrive as a light bulb moment that opens a window of opportunity for change, however it can also arrive in unexpected and disruptive circumstances, shaking us out of our complacency and pushing us to take actions that free us from

When in retrograde, the impulsive and volatile energy that brings us those important and necessary wake up calls, slows down and invites us to take conscious innovative actions to forge new ways of being and living that can liberate us from limiting perspectives. This energy when harnessed is particularly relevant to establishing liberation and equality for the greater collective.

Neptune in Retrograde.

- 25th June 23° Pisces – 1st December 20° Pisces

Neptune is the planet of creativity, dreams and imagination and as such plays a key role in manifestation. Being so dreamy, the influence of Neptunian energy opens us to divine guidance and Spiritual illumination supporting us on our pathway of the discovery of our true calling.

However, the duality of Neptune can also create an energetic in which we struggle to hold our boundaries, lose touch with reality, or become absorbed in illusion, creating a vulnerability to those who operate through delusion and deception.

When in retrograde, the Neptunian energy calls us to get real!

Bringing a level of illumination that offers a kind of Spiritual Reality check, we can see beyond the illusions that may have previously been holding us back, and use these powerful insights to initiate new pathways of creativity level to support and fuel our process of manifestation.

Pluto in Retrograde.

- **27th April 26° Capricorn – 6th October 24° Capricorn**

The energy of Pluto transforms through the natural cycle of death and re-birth and offers a powerful energetic of change. His intense volcanic energy takes us deep into the unconscious, showing us any shadows from the past that need to be released.

Pluto naturally invites us to harness the energy of personal reflection at its most powerful, bringing us an understanding of our psychological make-up so we may face our deepest issues, purify and release, emerging afresh with greater vitality and potency.

In our process of manifestation, Pluto retrograde energy invites us to surrender to that which we are shown and to reflect on those deep inner issues that rise from the unconscious desiring change and evolution.

This is not a time to hold onto or cling to the past. If some aspect of your world seems to be coming to an end, whether internal or external, such as any outdated thinking patterns or behaviors, an inappropriate or limiting belief, or an actual situation or person, let go gracefully and allow yourself to emerge into a space of new beginnings.

Chiron and the Consciousness of Healing.

Chiron in Retrograde.

- **27th April 26° Capricorn – 6th October 24° Capricorn**

Chiron embodies the classic architype of the wounded healer. In mythology he is depicted as half man and half beast, able to bring wisdom and to teach and heal others and yet he cannot heal himself.

Astrologically, Chiron is not a planet, but a comet, whose presence here is transient. Energetically it is said that his presence will create a rainbow bridge that will lead humanity to a higher plane of consciousness inviting us to stand in equality, not only alongside one another, but in unity with all of life. As an outer influence, his energy is slow moving and therefore can signify profound generational changes.

It is also interesting that many Tribal cultures hold legends that speak of all of the life on this planet arriving on the tail of a comet, validating the perspective that we all come from the same source and are all equal.

The retrograde energy of Chiron invites us to engage in a process of deep cleansing and release, laying the past to rest and stepping into a space of unity and higher vision. This is the kind of healing that carries the potential for us both as individuals and as a collective humanity to resolve long standing historical wounds that have spanned generations, bringing us deep and lasting healing in mind body and soul.

The Solstices and Equinoxes

At these pivotal moments in the natural cycles of time, it is as though the energy of the Earth pauses for breath. It is as though the space between heaven and earth becomes fluid, translucent and free of clutter. These shifts in time and space offer an extraordinary opportunity to achieve and access higher levels of consciousness and awareness.

During the four days either side of these powerful shifts we can often receive profound downloads of illumination, leading to an increase in our intuitive abilities, heightening our ability to channel and connect with source energy, divine inspiration and with the greater consciousness.

These pivotal moments in time bring extraordinary opportunities to reach a higher vision or viewpoint that can change our perceptions and perspectives, freeing us from limiting beliefs and bringing clarity of mind and new direction.

These periods are the perfect opportunity to engage in any spiritual practice that supports your personal growth and awareness and offer the ideal time to create ceremonies of appreciation, gratitude and celebration, as part of your manifestation process.

As well as the Solstices and the Equinoxes, during the year there are four other pivotal turning points which were understood and celebrated in the Celtic and Pagan traditions.

Exactly the same energetic principles apply and depending on whether you are in the northern or southern hemisphere, your ceremonies and celebrations at this time will vary, tuning you to the rhythm of the seasons of your own geographical area.

During these pivotal moments of natural transition, use this diary to check in with the incoming astrological energy, and allow yourself the time to meditate and take full advantage of the intensified energetic possibilities to enhance your personal process of manifestation.

TIGER EYE

My chosen crystal for the entire year of 2021 is Tiger Eye.

Throughout this journal, each month I have drawn upon specific crystals whose natural qualities offer support that align with the incoming astro-energy at that time. However, in terms of the overall flow of transformation and change over the coming year, Tiger Eye is without doubt the stone of the year, bringing an energy that will be supportive to us at every stage of our journey.

Tiger Eye is a stone of protection. It is said to bring luck to the wearer and creates a mental clarity that helps us to resolve any problems, particularly when our vision is shrouded in fog. F.O.G – Fear, Obligation or Guilt! It enhances strong willpower it is known to bring increased motivation and assist in overcoming any form of procrastination.

Personally, I find this powerful stone brings me courage and an inner strength that helps me to remain focused and steady with a clear mind. It is well worth carrying if you are going to enter conversations that require a strength of conviction. It is also a wonderful energy to draw on when I am needing to find solutions to a particular problem. When I sit with my Tiger Eye Angel at my side during a meditation it seems to create a pathway for the answers to arrive.

Welcome to January 2021

January. The New is Calling.

January looks to bring us a dynamic and intense beginning to our New Year. The warrior planet of Mars enters Taurus on the 6th, moving into alignment with Uranus, the great awakener and instigator of sudden changes. Take time to relax and review during the first week of this powerful month before the energy rises and intensifies.

Mercury, the winged messenger of the gods and ruler of communication, enters Aquarius on the eighth and in the buildup to the New Moon on the 13th will align with both Saturn and Jupiter. In terms of manifestation and personal empowerment, this collaboration offers us a magical window of opportunity to focus our minds on the kind of connections and negotiations that we will need to create to find solutions to the challenges that we face both individually and as a collective humanity.

The New Moon on the 13th aligns with Pluto, the planet of transformation, change and rebirth. They in turn form an intense relationship with Mars and Uranus. The energetic of the New Moon will always call us to sow seeds and create new beginnings and these powerful and dynamic connections have the potential to create situations that challenge us, but this is not without purpose. These powerful influences are here to highlight any outdated views and perceptions that no longer serve us.

As we journey through the month, the pressure holds its own.

On the 19th the Sun enters Aquarius. Use the energy to focus on ways to manifest your personal hopes, aspirations, dreams and desires. This is a time to seek out those whose values align with your own. Collaboration will be needed to support the actions necessary to become a consciously active participant in this year of change.

The pressure is building and continues to do so as we move into the energy of the Full Moon on the 28th. Structures may crumble... the new is calling, whether we like it or not!

When Mercury moves into retrograde on the 30th we are called to reflect and review. If disruption occurs, and difficulties arise, trust that a delay can retrospectively prove to be providential... even if it doesn't feel like it at the time!

As I write this, I am reminded of the Tarot Card of the Wheel of Fortune. In essence this card speaks of destiny and of the wheel of our life's experiences turning, however this card does not present us as passive victims to a life that is happening to us. Whilst circumstances and events that are out of our control clearly do take place around us, this card simultaneously recognizes and acknowledges that nothing is set in stone, and from a karmic perspective, we have choices in the way in which we respond to situations and as such we are active participants in the making of our own destiny.

This is a month to truly acknowledge that what we think, speak, and do, is actively creating our external reality. Much may be revealed to us over the next few weeks, both individually and collectively, and however challenging this may be, we are being shown our unique and individual pathway to participate in humanities transition into a new age.

The Power of Collective Prayer

As the energy builds in intensity and we move towards our first period of collective prayer in February, please spread the word.

In these pivotal times of change we can collectively center ourselves in the higher vibration of the Saturn, Uranus energetic, creating openings that lead to innovative, new and peaceful solutions.

**First Collective Prayer for 2021
February 16th – 24th inclusive.**

ORANGE CALCITE

In alignment with the dynamic astro-energy of January I found myself instantly drawn to the energized and dynamic healing qualities of Orange Calcite.

Known as the 'Enhancement Stone', Orange Calcite, like other calcites is said to have powerful healing attributes. Associated with the energy of the Sun and the element of Fire, this stunning crystal is said to realign us with renewed vitality, energizing our primary life force.

In my own experience, I can recommend that if you are struggling to feel the confidence to step into your fullest potential or need some assistance to remove inner blocks to discovering and fulfilling your life's purpose then this stunning crystal brings just the energy needed to support you in this process.

The New Moon in January
Wishes and Intentions

12th/13th Jan - New Moon in Capricorn

This is an incredibly dynamic New Moon, and albeit a little intense, it is loaded with the potential for us to co-create the kind of changes that we wish to see in the world.

Our first New Moon of 2021 sits in conjunction with Pluto, the planet of renewal, re-birth and transformation. Saturn, whose energy has been calling us to de-structure in order to re-structure, aligns with the expansive Jupiter and Mercury, the winged messenger of the gods, who in turn makes a strong connection with Mars, the warrior planet, Lilith, Goddess of desire and Uranus the great awakener.

Use this New Moon Energy to make wishes that align your personal goals and desire for success and recognition, with your calling and your purpose. Give yourself full permission to listen to those desires that call from your heart, and if disruption occurs trust that it is happening with purpose, bringing important and necessary information to highlight the steps needed to guide you towards new pathways of greater alignment.

In your New Moon ceremonies write down your 10 wishes and open yourself to receive the guidance that you need to highlight the next steps on your pathway of manifestation.

To engage with the New Moon energy at its most powerful, be sure to write your wishes down during the 8 hours following the exact time of the New Moon in your location.

- 12th January - Los Angeles 21.00
- 13th January – New York 00.00
- 13th January - London 05.00
- 13th January – Sydney 16.00
- 13th January – Auckland 18.00

My Ten New Moon Wishes

1

2

3

4

5

6

7

8

9

10

-- Wishes and Dreams --

The Full Moon in January

28th/29th Jan - Full Moon in Leo

The Full Moon occurs when the Sun and the Moon sit directly opposite one another. It is the time in each month when the Moon has gathered light and energy from the Sun and shines at her brightest, illuminating all that needs to be seen.

Use this time each month to meditate and request illumination and guidance to support your manifestations.

It is also the very best time of the month to place your Crystals outside overnight to recharge in the powerful light of the Moon.

The Full Moon in Leo will highlight those areas of your life that deserve to be celebrated to the full, encouraging you to be confident. She will also illuminate any areas of your life where your ego is in conflict or out of balance with your heart.

Each month place some rainwater or spring water in a bowl and leave it out overnight to absorb the energy of the Full Moon. Do NOT use a plastic bowl! Use glass or earthenware or any container whose fundamental ingredients come from a natural source. Collect the water afterwards and store it in a jar.

Use the Moon Water in any of your ceremonies that need a turbo charged boost of abundant and confident Leo energy.

- 28th January - Los Angeles 11.16
- 28th January – New York 14.16
- 28th January - London 19.16
- 29th January – Sydney 06.16
- 29th January – Auckland 08.16

January 2021

Journaling and Notes

Journaling and Notes

Journaling and Notes

Journaling and Notes

Journaling and Notes

--------------------------------- January 2021 ---------------------------------

Welcome to February 2021

February. The Pressure Builds… Leading to Potential Productivity!

The intense and dynamic flavor of January continues into the first two weeks of February, with pressure building up to a square between Saturn, the planet of structure and the bearer of karmic lessons and the lighting spirit of Uranus, the great awakener, exact between the 16th and the 24th and at its most powerful on the 17th.

In terms of manifestation, I personally think the best way to handle this kind of incoming dynamic energy is to practice the 'Art of Allowing'. As the month progresses we will reach a pivotal turning point of potential revelation when Mercury stations direct on the 21st sitting midway between Saturn and Jupiter giving us an opportunity to carry our learning from the month, and indeed our learning from the past, into our vision of the future that we wish to co-create and manifest.

The overall energy of February calls us to develop tolerance and to truly value and appreciate our differences. With Mercury in retrograde, be sure to stand back and take time to review and evaluate anything and everything that is happening around you. These energetics call us to appreciate difference and to develop tolerance and flexibility in the way that we navigate our personal responsibilities, particularly in relationship to others, but also of course in relationship with ourselves.

The New Moon on the 11th in Aquarius invites us to align our wishes with a long-term vision for a collective and united humanity. Mercury, Venus, Jupiter, also in Aquarius, form a powerful and dynamic relationship with the warrior planet Mars. This energetic is softened by the influence of dreamy Neptune creating an opportunity to step into our own dreamtime and imagine the kind of future that we wish to create.

A New Moon is effectively a sacred marriage between the Sun and the Moon who come together, their energies uniting. At the moment they meet, the energetic power of raw creativity is particularly potent. Their sacred union in Aquarius this month naturally invites us to embody dreams and visions that speak of sustainable possibilities for the greater collective, and this collective extends beyond humanity embracing all of life, of which we are an integral part.

The Sun enters Pisces on the 18th supporting us in sustaining the visions that we have created during our New Moon dreamtime. On the 21st Mercury stations direct midway between karmic Saturn and Jupiter, the bringer of expansive energy, new opportunities, new possibilities and newfound hope and optimism. This positioning creates a pivotal moment in which the energy invites us to take all of our learning historically and weave it into our future dreams to create a new foundation of wealth and prosperity built on these values that can truly sustain a higher vision.

In the last week of February, the energy of the Full Moon in Virgo on the 27th invites us to take practical pragmatic steps to initiate the creation of the best possible conditions for our dreams to grow into fruition.

The First Collective Prayer for 2021
February 16th – 24th inclusive.

Saturn, the planet of structure and the bearer of karmic lessons and the lighting spirit of Uranus, the great awakener square up together this month.

In the intensity of this collaboration please join me for a minute of silent prayer at 7pm each day during this period. Let us hold the higher vibration of this energetic and channel the extraordinary potential of this energy into a collective vision of a united humanity.

As we lean into the astro-energy of February calling for truth and equality the voice of Lapis Lazuli came forward.

Be the change that you wish to see in the world! Stand in your truth and find your voice! This magnificent stone radiates the energy of the Spiritual Warrior striving to walk a pathway of authenticity.

Lapis Lazuli is a powerful stone of self-expression. Said to reveal our inner truth through self-awareness, this extraordinary stone is said to encourage us to uphold honesty and integrity whilst observing ourselves and others through the eyes of compassion.

New Moon Wishes and Intentions

11th/12th Feb - New Moon in Aquarius

The potent creative energy of this New Moon in Aquarius invites us to stand back and to walk tall, and regardless of what may be taking place around us, calls us to hold faith and to dream into a higher vision for the future, both individually and collectively.

The Aquarian New Moon energy is particularly powerful in supporting wishes that enable the kinds of relationships and friendships that resonate with a higher calling creating networks with likeminded souls who belief in humanitarian principles and strive to live and work in unity.

Whether you are looking to build alliances with new work colleagues, create friendships of greater consciousness, or you are seeking to manifest a Soulmate union, the energetic of this moon is perfect for setting wishes and intentions that not only align you with your true purpose, but also call in collaborative connections that support this, both personally and professionally.

In your meditations at this time, be open to receiving the kinds of ideas and insights that lead to unconventional and 'thinking out of the box' solutions. Alongside your list of wishes, you may want to create a vision board that reaches far into the future.

In your New Moon ceremonies write down your 10 wishes and open yourself to receive the guidance that you need to highlight the next steps on your pathway of manifestation.

To engage with the New Moon energy at its most powerful, be sure to write your wishes down during the 8 hours following the exact time of the New Moon in your location.

- 11th February - Los Angeles 11.05
- 11th February – New York 14.05
- 11th February - London 19.05
- 12th February – Sydney 06.05
- 12th February – Auckland 08.05

My Ten New Moon Wishes

1

2

3

4

5

6

7

8

9

10

-- Wishes and Dreams --

The Full Moon in February

27th February - Full Moon in Virgo

The Full Moon occurs when the Sun and the Moon sit directly opposite one another. It is the time in each month when the Moon has gathered light and energy from the Sun and shines at her brightest, illuminating all that needs to be seen.

Use this time each month to meditate and request illumination and guidance to support your manifestations.

It is also the very best time of the month to place your Crystals outside overnight to recharge in the powerful light of the Moon.

The Full Moon in Virgo will highlight those areas of your life that are defined by the combination of both practicality as well as an active mind. Illumination may arrive to show you exactly what steps you need to take in real terms to support your journey of manifestation. She will also highlight any areas of your life where perfectionism is holding you back!

Each month place some rainwater or spring water in a bowl and leave it out overnight to absorb the energy of the Full Moon. Do NOT use a plastic bowl! Use glass or earthenware or any container whose fundamental ingredients come from a natural source. Collect the water afterwards and store it in a jar.

Use the Moon Water in any of your ceremonies that need a turbo charged boost of clear thinking and practical action.

- 27th February - Los Angeles 00.17
- 27th February – New York 03.17
- 27th February - London 08.17
- 27th February – Sydney 19.17
- 27th February – Auckland 21.17

-- February 2021 --

Journaling and Notes

-------------------------------- February 2021 ---------------------------------

February 2021

Journaling and Notes

Journaling and Notes

Journaling and Notes

Journaling and Notes

Journaling and Notes

Reflections from February

Welcome to March 2021

March 2021. The Energy Starts to Lift. Evaluate your Visions!

Following an intense beginning to the year, the energetic turning point in February is continued into March and we begin to see a levelling out and a lifting of the pressure that was so prevalent at the start of the year.

The New Moon on the 13th aligns with dreamy Neptune who in turn joins forces with Venus. Collectively they hold a beautiful energetic of love, light, compassion and creativity.

Open yourself to receive insights and illuminations of the highest order.

In terms of manifestation any changes that we wish to initiate at this time have the potential to gather energy and to flow into being with ease, however, the flow of Neptunian energy, like the oceans, carries immense power and can change in an instant. Waves can gently lap at our feet and yet in the next moment an undercurrent can sweep us off our feet.

Given that the influence of Neptune is one of deep, watery, dreamy power, if you find yourself swamped by insights and illuminations to the point of feeling quite overwhelmed, slow down... take your time... and allow yourself to receive.

Become an observer of your experiences, particularly of your dreams. Use this journal to keep a record of all that you are shown, and as the month progresses all will become clear.

The Sun enters Aries on the 20th March signifying the start of a new astrological year.

At this time, in combination with the energy of the equinox when the earth pauses for breath, we have the potential to tap into profound moments of insight and guidance.

Be sure to keep your journal by your side during your mediations and make notes of any insights that come to you at this time and use them to begin to make constructive plans for the future.

The Full Moon in Libra on the 28th makes a heavenly trine with karmic Saturn, motivated Mars and the North Node, signifying an extraordinary opportunity to implement and initiate changes and steps in our manifestation.

With the input of Uranus, the great awakener, whose energy clears the way for the new, if anything occurs around the Full Moon period to give you a nudge into a space of possibility, trust that this is destiny calling.

The Power of Collective Prayer

Thank you for joining me in the one minute of silent prayer during February. Together we really can make a difference.

I look forward to reconnecting with you again in June.

Namaste

As we journey through March 2021 and intensity of the astro-energy lifts, opening ourselves to the flowing energetics of love and creativity, we call upon the magnificent properties of Aqua Calcite.

Divine Guidance!

Opening our crown chakra and third eye Aqua Calcite is said to open pathways of communication with our Spirit Guides. This is an extraordinary crystal to sit with in meditation, particularly around the Full and New Moons when we open ourselves to divine guidance, seeking support from a higher consciousness and universal law. Freeing us from the limitations of inappropriate beliefs and attitudes, it is said to enhance and amplify the energy of any other crystals and is frequently used for healing in all areas of mind body and Soul.

New Moon Wishes and Intentions

13th March - New Moon in Pisces

This New Moon is particularly potent for setting wishes of transformation, the letting go of the old and the birthing of the new, the energy is ripe to manifest any aspect of our lives that we wish to transform, reinvent or rebirth. Focus your wishes on anything that you wish to bring to fruition and birth into the world. Open yourself to receive divine guidance on your pathway of manifestation.

This New Moon is also particularly powerful if any form of emotional healing is needed and for setting wishes that release the past and make way for the new to emerge. Align your wishes with those desires that bring you deep happiness and peace and spiritual wellbeing.

If your wishes include career choices to make the most of the Piscean energy and choose wishes that support a career pathway that brings deep emotional fulfillment.

If you have been hurt in love or relationship, this New Moon is perfect to wish for a relationship that re-establishes trust and is worthy of a deep soul connection.

You may also want to include wishes that support you in letting go of confusion, habits of procrastination, or any self-defeating thinking patterns and behaviors.

In your New Moon ceremonies write down your 10 wishes and open yourself to receive the guidance that you need to highlight the next steps on your pathway of manifestation. To engage with the New Moon energy at its most powerful, be sure to write your wishes down during the 8 hours following the exact time of the New Moon in your location.

- **13th March - Los Angeles 02.21**
- **13th March – New York 05.21**
- **13th March - London 10.21**
- **13th March – Sydney 21.21**
- **13th March – Auckland 23.21**

My Ten New Moon Wishes

1

2

3

4

5

6

7

8

9

10

The Full Moon in March

28th/28th March - Full Moon in Libra

The Full Moon occurs when the Sun and the Moon sit directly opposite one another. It is the time in each month when the Moon has gathered light and energy from the Sun and shines at her brightest, illuminating all that needs to be seen.

Use this time each month to meditate and request illumination and guidance to support your manifestations.

It is also the very best time of the month to place your Crystals outside overnight to recharge in the powerful light of the Moon.

The Full Moon in Libra will highlight any areas of our lives that are out of balance, particularly within partnerships and relationships, but this doesn't necessarily mean conflict. She will also send us illuminations to show us the most balanced and harmonious route to fix the problem.

Each month place some rainwater or spring water in a bowl and leave it out overnight to absorb the energy of the Full Moon. Do NOT use a plastic bowl! Use glass or earthenware or any container whose fundamental ingredients come from a natural source. Collect the water afterwards and store it in a jar.

Use the Moon Water in any of your ceremonies to add a powerful extra dose of balance, harmony and love.

- 28th March - Los Angeles 01.48
- 28th March – New York 14.48
- 28th March - London 19.48
- 29th March – Sydney 05.48
- 29th March – Auckland 07.48

----------------------------------- March 2021 --

Journaling and Notes

------------------------------- March 2021 -----------------------

Journaling and Notes

-------------------------------- March 2021 --------------------------------

------------------------------- March 2021 -------------------------------

Journaling and Notes

Journaling and Notes

-------------------------- March 2021 --------------------------

Reflections from March

-- Journaling & Notes --

78

Welcome to April 2021

April. Revelations, Healing and New Beginnings.

The overall dynamics of this month highlight the power of joining forces and collaboration, however this month may also show us how this power can be misused.

In the first two weeks, as we move towards the manifestation opportunities of the new Moon in Aries on the 12th, use this time to notice those areas of your life that require healing. And be mindful to recognize the connections between inner and outer. If we are seeing external circumstances that need reparation and healing then this is also a mirror or representation of deeper inner issues that we each can investigate and address on a personal way, thus contributing to the collective healing and expanding consciousness of humanity as a whole.

The New Moon in Aries is primed for change and transformation and remember, friction can give us traction!

If something in your life is calling for change, use the illuminations and insights that were passed to and through you during March to evaluate the full scope of your conscious choices, leading to an empowered course of mindful action and direction. Despite some pressure from Pluto, the bringer of transformation and rebirth, our beautiful New Moon flows harmoniously with the masculine go-getting Warrior energy of Mars aided by the expansive and optimistic energy of Jupiter.

With Neptune also bringing a worthy contribution to the overall dynamic, if you find yourself feeling emotional at this time, learn to listen to your emotions as a navigational tool and the bringers of valuable information.

And likewise, should anything emerge from deep within your unconscious, remember that it is only when we look into the shadows that we can truly clear away the old and make space to reconnect with the light and bring in the new.

On the 19th the Sun enters Taurus, emphasizing our physical wellbeing and self-care. If the exuberant energy of the New Moon has left you feeling a little physically or emotionally tired, be sure to take time out and be conscious in the management of your schedule.

Building up to the Full moon in Scorpio on the 27th the energetics suggest a time of disclosures and revelations with issues being raised and important information brought to light. From the perspective of manifestation consider this a period of time when we are being given an opportunity to identify any areas within our personal scope of influence that really is calling for change.

EMERALD & GREEN CALCITE

In a powerful month when much may be shown to us in the calling of change and transformation, we call again to the great healing of the Calcite family. This month we will draw on the wisdom and energy of Green and Emerald Calcite.

Emerald Calcite is said to clear stagnant and blocked energy, freeing us to break away from any old relationship habits and patterns that do not work in our interest. Slightly different in color to Green Calcite, they hold very similar properties. Green Calcite is sometimes known as a memory stone. The energy of both align with the Heart Chakra and the Higher Heart Chakra, supporting healing within the emotional, spiritual, physical and mental realms, thus offering opportunity to assist in the healing and resolution of any historic or challenging memories.

I find that when I sit with this gorgeous crystal, I automatically begin to view my situation differently, and in overriding past perspectives, I can hold past memories in a far more objective and forgiving light. The two in unison make a powerful team in overcoming any issues from the past that are clinging or hindering your personal growth and evolution.

New Moon Wishes and Intentions

11th/12th April - New Moon in Aries

This new moon in Aries is absolutely primed for change and transformation.

A crucial aspect of learning to master the art of manifestation process lies in our ability to recognize that when we feel fired up about something, whether this is something that we absolutely love or something that we truly dislike, in both instances, our passion is firing an energetic intent into the universe. In essence what this means in real terms is that when we dwell on those things that we don't want as much as those that we do, then we are inadvertently investing a huge emotional charge into something that we don't wish to create and as such can actually be sabotaging our ability to manifest those wishes and dreams that we do wish to birth into the world and make real.

A Prayer is a focused thought... An intention is a focused thought... A worry or a dislike is also a focused thought! Use the energy of this new moon to create wishes that focus on the manifestation of healing for any former hurts that still trouble you.

Use your recognition of these to give greater and more precise definition to anything and everything on your wish list that makes your heart soar and is a true reflection of all that makes you happy and connects you with the passions and desires that are true to your heart.

In your New Moon ceremonies write down your 10 wishes and open yourself to receive the guidance that you need to highlight the next steps on your pathway of manifestation. To engage with the New Moon energy at its most powerful, be sure to write your wishes down during the 8 hours following the exact time of the New Moon in your location.

- 11th April - Los Angeles 19.30
- 11th April – New York 22.30
- 12th April - London 03.30
- 12th April – Sydney 12.30
- 12th April – Auckland 14.30

My Ten New Moon Wishes

1

2

3

4

5

6

7

8

9

10

-- Wishes and Dreams --

The Full Moon in April

26th/27th April – Super Full Moon in Scorpio

The Full Moon occurs when the Sun and the Moon sit directly opposite one another. It is the time in each month when the Moon has gathered light and energy from the Sun and shines at her brightest, illuminating all that needs to be seen.

Use this time each month to meditate and request illumination and guidance to support your manifestations.

It is also the very best time of the month to place your Crystals outside overnight to recharge in the powerful light of the Moon.

A Super Full Moon occurs when the Moon is at her closest point to the Earth which means this Full Moon in Scorpio will have an extra added charge to her energy. If you have something that you need to release, this is THE Full Moon to do it on. A Scorpio Full Moon will bring anything to the surface that needs to be seen, processed and if necessary, laid to rest.

If you find yourself feeling particularly emotional, trust that this Full Moon is highlighting your deeper inner feelings and wishes to help you to find a voice.

Each month place some rainwater or spring water in a bowl and leave it out overnight to absorb the energy of the Full Moon. Do NOT use a plastic bowl! Use glass or earthenware or any container whose fundamental ingredients come from a natural source. Collect the water afterwards and store it in a jar.

Use the Moon Water in any of your ceremonies to cut cords and to release the past.

- 26th April - Los Angeles 20.31
- 26th April – New York 23.31
- 27th April - London 04.31
- 27th April – Sydney 13.31
- 27th April – Auckland 15.31

April 2021

April 2021

Journaling and Notes

Journaling and Notes

April 2021

Journaling and Notes

Journaling and Notes

-- Journaling & Notes --

Welcome to May 2021

May 2021. The Emergence of a New Age. How do we want to handle this?

The overall energetic of May suggests that we will see a tension between the old and the new, and the inevitable pressure that arises as we work out how to balance the need for freedom and liberation alongside an ownership of our personal responsibility and recognition of the consequences of our actions.

With the New Moon in earthy Taurus on the 11th May we are offered an invitation to take informed actions that will bring about constructive changes.

At the time of this New Moon, the restructuring energy of Saturn and changeable energy of Uranus edge closer and closer together, with Saturn also forming a strong karmic influence with the North Node.

The influence of Chiron, the wounded healer, is also particularly strong in the overall dynamics. Chiron, half man half beast, is said to play a key role in creating a rainbow bridge of healing that will lead humanity into a new age of higher consciousness where we can learn through peace rather than continual adversity.

With Pluto the planet of transformation connecting favorably with the Moon herself, this New Moon in Taurus suggests an incredibly fruitful time to sow seeds of change.

For these changes to emerge and blossom a balance will need to be found between the needs of the individual and the needs of the whole. When I use the term 'the whole', this extends way beyond the needs of our collective humanity; we are also called to embrace the needs of our beautiful planet and all of the life that she sustains.

Jupiter enters Pisces on the 13th and the Sun enters Gemini on the 20th bringing the energy of collaboration to the fore and with the connection between Uranus and Saturn intensifying, when we reach the Full Moon Eclipse in Sagittarius on the 26th the added expansive energy of Jupiter invites us to align with a spiritual vision that embodies the unity of all of life.

Eclipse season is traditionally known to create energetic portals of energy that like a timeline, link the past, the present, and the future, opening windows of opportunity for Karmic resolution. We can expect powerful opportunities for change at this time! Now in the shadow period of the 29th May Mercury

Retrograde, if a delay or hold up occurs, trust that this will have purpose, even if we cannot yet see the bigger picture.

The Power of Collective Prayer

As we move towards June, the intensity of the Saturn, Uranus connection rises again.

I look ford to joining with you again for our second period of collective silent prayer.

Please spread the word.

**Second Collective Prayer for 2021
June 13th – 17th inclusive.**

In a month where the astro-energy offers huge potential for manifestation whilst also calling us to find balance and sow seeds of equality and higher purpose we link with the gorgeous energy of Moonstone.

Moonstone.

Moonstone invites us to open our hearts and to love without judgment. It is associated with fertility and sensuality connecting us with the inner goddess that sits within us all, heightening our intuition, and clearing and cleansing our mind from any negative emotions, especially those connected to our relationships. Used in meditation, particularly at the time of the New Moon, it is said to enhance our powers of manifestation. Moonstone brings a wonderful energy into any New Moon ceremonies associated with our dreams, wishes and desires reminding us of the Miracles that surround us and of the infinite support of Spirit and the Universe.

New Moon Wishes and Intentions

11th/12th May - New Moon in Taurus

In a month that invites us to find a way of living that can balance our own needs alongside the wellbeing of all of life, including our amazing Planet Earth, the dynamics of the New Moon in Taurus offer us a stunning opportunity to align ourselves with the coming of a new age and actively sow seeds that support the fertility of a balanced future in which our physical, emotional and material needs are met without detriment to others or the Earth.

New Moon wishes in Taurus are traditionally associated with our physical wellbeing, our possessions and our material wealth. The energy also supports us in building self-worth and to develop patience, perseverance, determination and self-acceptance.

If you struggle with any aspect of low self-esteem and find it hard to stand up for those things that you believe in then this moon is perfect to set wishes that send out a request to receive help in this area of your life. Likewise, if you have any physical health issues this is a great New Moon to request help and assistance in this area of your life.

If you are struggling to manifest healthy finances and material wealth this is also a great New Moon to place your wishes into the universe.

In your New Moon ceremonies write down your 10 wishes and open yourself to receive the guidance that you need to highlight the next steps on your pathway of manifestation. To engage with the New Moon energy at its most powerful, be sure to write your wishes down during the 8 hours following the exact time of the New Moon in your location.

- 11th May - Los Angeles 11.59
- 11th May – New York 14.59
- 11th May - London 19.59
- 12th May – Sydney 04.59
- 12th May – Auckland 06.59

My Ten New Moon Wishes

1

2

3

4

5

6

7

8

9

10

The Full Moon in May

26th May – Super Full Moon Eclipse in Sagittarius

The Full Moon occurs when the Sun and the Moon sit directly opposite one another. It is the time in each month when the Moon has gathered light and energy from the Sun and shines at her brightest, illuminating all that needs to be seen.

Use this time each month to meditate and request illumination and guidance to support your manifestations.

It is also the very best time of the month to place your Crystals outside overnight to recharge in the powerful light of the Moon.

The Super Full Moon Eclipse in Sagittarius offers brings an amazing opportunity to access portals of energy that can significantly aid our process of manifestation. Like a timeline connecting past, present and future we can trust this expansive and freedom loving Full Moon will illuminate the steps needed to fulfill our dreams, wishes and desires whilst also supporting us in letting go of any limiting beliefs that may have previously been holding us back.

Each month place some rainwater or spring water in a bowl and leave it out overnight to absorb the energy of the Full Moon. Do NOT use a plastic bowl! Use glass or earthenware or any container whose fundamental ingredients come from a natural source. Collect the water afterwards and store it in a jar.

Use the Moon Water in any of your ceremonies to add a super charge in the manifestation of your ambitions, your dreams, your wishes and your desires.

- **26th May - Los Angeles 04.13**
- **26th May – New York 07.13**
- **26th May - London 12.13**
- **26th May – Sydney 21.13**
- **26th May – Auckland 23.13**

May 2021

Journaling and Notes

Journaling and Notes

-- May 2021 --

Journaling and Notes

Journaling and Notes

Journaling and Notes

Journaling and Notes

May 2021

Reflections from May

-- Journaling & Notes --

Welcome to June 2021

June 2021. A Pivotal Turning Point.

The energy of June looks to herald a pivotal turning point in a year of unprecedented change and accelerated evolution.

This month the incoming astro-energy is dominated by the powerful squaring of Uranus, the great awakener and bringer of sudden changes, and the re-structuring energy of karmic Saturn. Given the intensity of this connection, be sure to take time to prioritize your self-care, in mind, body, emotion and soul. If you are in the northern hemisphere take full advantage of the long evenings and be sure to find time just to be. Likewise, if you are in the southern hemisphere, fuel yourself with winter food and be sure to tuck into the dark evenings creating space for reflection and make time just to be.

With Eclipse season at its peak and Mercury now in retrograde until the 22nd, if events do not run smoothly, take this as a sign to slow down, reflect and potentially reconsider before pushing into further action.

The New Moon Eclipse in Gemini on the 10th brings an interesting mix of energies. The Moon herself links favorably with Saturn suggesting a healthy opportunity to restructure, however she also connects less harmoniously with Neptune whose energy in turn flows easily with both Pluto and Mars. And with the calling for restructure from Saturn firmly attached to Uranus, the bringer of sudden revolutionary change, if you find yourself facing decisions and are uncertain which way to go, try not to rush!

Take your time and meditate. Eclipse season is the perfect time to receive higher guidance. It is highly likely under the current influences that the answers you seek may be unconventional and come from unexpected sources. If you feel a sense of urgency, use this energy to consider the best course of action from a longer-term perspective.

The Sun enters Cancer on the Solstice on the 21st creating a four-day window of reflection. (See page 27 for Solstice Information) and Mercury stations direct on the 22nd linking in with karmic Saturn for the Full Moon in Capricorn on the 24th enhancing the potential for positive communications that draw on our reflections and the learning from the year so far.

In the dynamic energetics of the Full Moon, the masculine warrior planet of Mars joins the already powerful connection between Uranus and Saturn pushing us to take action. Add to the mix a strong opposition between Pluto and Venus; if a relationship to a situation, person or circumstance, or an attitude or thinking pattern or behavior seems to be breaking down, let it go gracefully.

This pivotal month asks us to embrace the changes we are shown, believe in new and better future, and lean into a space of trust.

The Second Collective Prayer for 2021
June 13th – 17th inclusive.

Saturn, the planet of structure and the bearer of karmic lessons and the lighting spirit of Uranus, the great awakener square up again this month.

In the intensity of this collaboration please join me for a minute of silent prayer at 7pm each day during this period. Let us hold the higher vibration of this energetic and channel the extraordinary potential of this energy into a collective vision of a united humanity opening ourselves to receive the guidance that we need to find innovative and creative solutions to pave the way to new and sustainable ways of living.

CHERRY QUARTZ

At this pivotal turning point in the year, when the Earth pauses for breath before moving into a new cycle and a new phase of being, we call upon the energy of Cherry Quartz. The profound energetic shifts that take place at the Solstices and the Equinoxes can cause us to feel a little bit disorientated. I have found that carrying my little Cherry Quartz Angel with me during these times seems to keep me in line with the energy flow and supports me in keeping my long term visions in mind, whilst also enabling me to see where any adjustments might be needed in my current course of action.

Cherry quartz is said to increase our overall energy and bring a shift in our fortune, releasing us from any form of stagnant or stuck situation and enabling us to move forwards and to better any situation. My little angel just radiates energy. It feels buoyant, positive and overflowing with optimism.

New Moon Wishes and Intentions

10th June - New Moon Eclipse in Gemini

Eclipse season is known to open portals of awareness that span time, enabling us to connect with the potential resolution of the past, in order to forge new pathways into the future.

The energy of a Gemini New Moon will naturally lend itself to wishes that connect to better avenues of communication, making and sustaining positive connections, clarity of thinking, effective listening, awareness of options and opportunities and our capacity to learn from experience.

The planetary collaborations of this New Moon Eclipse invite us to understand change and uncertainty from a spiritual perspective. With the overall dynamics of June presenting us with a pivotal turning point on our evolutionary pathway into a new age, whether from a personal perspective, for others around you, or for the greater consciousness of humanity, this is a perfect New Moon to set wishes for the healing of both mind and emotion. If you struggle with anxiety in the face of uncertainty, make wishes to change this, easily and soon. If you are seeking greater clarity of thought and direction make wishes that ask for signs, signals and guidance that is easy to follow. If you struggle to have your voice, make wishes that request smooth communications in all of your dealings with others.

In your New Moon ceremonies write down your 10 wishes and open yourself to receive the guidance that you need to highlight the next steps on your pathway of manifestation. To engage with the New Moon energy at its most powerful, be sure to write your wishes down during the 8 hours following the exact time of the New Moon in your location.

- 10th June - Los Angeles 03.52
- 10th June – New York 06.52
- 10th June - London 11.52
- 10th June – Sydney 20.52
- 10th June – Auckland 22.52

My Ten New Moon Wishes

1

2

3

4

5

6

7

8

9

10

The Full Moon in June

24th/25th June – Full Moon in Capricorn

The Full Moon occurs when the Sun and the Moon sit directly opposite one another. It is the time in each month when the Moon has gathered light and energy from the Sun and shines at her brightest, illuminating all that needs to be seen.

Use this time each month to meditate and request illumination and guidance to support your manifestations.

It is also the very best time of the month to place your Crystals outside overnight to recharge in the powerful light of the Moon.

The Full Moon in Capricorn will highlight aspects of our lives where we can benefit from learning to use our emotions as a source of empowerment, illuminating a pathway of learning that will help us to build resilience, endurance, self-discipline and the staying power to complete a project.

Each month place some rainwater or spring water in a bowl and leave it out overnight to absorb the energy of the Full Moon. Do NOT use a plastic bowl! Use glass or earthenware or any container whose fundamental ingredients come from a natural source. Collect the water afterwards and store it in a jar.

Use this Moon Water in any of your ceremonies of manifestation that need an extra boost of turbo charged staying power, to bring resilience and durability.

And don't forget to put your Crystals out to recharge as well!

- 24th June - Los Angeles 11.39
- 24th June – New York 14.39
- 24th June - London 19.39
- 25th June – Sydney 04.39
- 25th June – Auckland 06.39

My Full Moon Insights and Illuminations

Journaling and Notes

June 2021

Journaling and Notes

Journaling and Notes

Journaling and Notes

Journaling and Notes

-- Journaling & Notes --

Welcome to July 2021

July 2021. A Space of In Between.

With four major planets, Pluto, Saturn, Jupiter and Neptune all now in Retrograde, at a time when we are also being called to take actions that initiate the new, a fair degree of tension can be expected during this month.

Although the New Moon in Cancer on the 10th aligns favorably with both Neptune and Uranus, offering the potential for sudden and unexpected moments of insight and illumination, the overall energy is still dominated by the Saturn Uranus connection now in a challenging relationship with both Mars and Venus, the masculine and feminine warrior planets, both in Leo.

With Saturn now in retrograde we might expect to see a tension between the old and the new, with any resistance to change surfacing, particularly in any areas that are demanding a greater degree of recognition and equality.

The union of Venus and Mars is exact on the 13th. What we do with this energetic is in many ways a question of personal perspective and personal choice.

If compromises are needed in any form of negotiation, be sure to take all parties needs into account.

With the Sun entering Leo on the 22nd we are asked to remember that dominance is never helpful in negotiations, however, it is also important to hold our boundaries in the face of something that is genuinely inappropriate or unacceptable.

The energy builds to the Full Moon in Aquarius on the 24th aligning with Pluto, the planet of re-birth and transformation, now in retrograde. With the tension between Mercury and Pluto softened by the higher spiritual energy of Neptune, if any negotiations were previously seeming to be going nowhere, there is now an opportunity to birth decisive and clear solutions that come from a higher perspective.

From the perspective of manifestation, it can serve us to stand back and view the energy of July from the perspective of a space of 'in between'.

We have been systematically shown all that needs to be changed in order to bring about a sustainable future for humanity, however we have yet to forge plans that can be implemented to manifest this possibility into real form, and as always, in the face of radical change, there will inevitably be a degree of resistance, especially from those whose world had previously thrived on the basis of the old systems of power.

The Power of Collective Prayer

Thank you for joining me in the one minute of silent prayer during June.

Together we really can make a difference.

I look forward to reconnecting with you again in December.

Namaste

In this incredibly powerful month when we find ourselves occupying the space that sits between the old and the new and the push and pull energetic of the to take action verses the need to be still and to contemplate, I found myself drawn to profound energy of Amazonite.

For me, Amazonite feels akin to the Tarot Card of Justice. It has a sense of gravity about it, calling us to stand in truth and walk a pathway of justice, equality and fairness. And yet despite its powerful presence it radiates calm, coupled with an inner peace and an inner sense of deep wellbeing. As such it is an essential crystal in the tool kit of the Spiritual Warrior.

It is said that the energy of Amazonite enables us to stand back and view our situation from all angles. Associated with the Heart Chakra it is said to enhance our ability to manifest universal love. In healing it is said to soothe trauma and to release toxins associated with our emotions and the nervous system.

New Moon Wishes and Intentions

9th/10th July - New Moon in Cancer

The energy of a Cancer New Moon will naturally invite us to focus on wishes that connect to our sense of belonging, our home and our family. Given the overall dynamic of July the Cancerian energy will also support us in making wishes that help us to overcome our insecurities and ground us in our ability to nurture and invest in new beginnings.

If you are someone who feels particularly vulnerable during times of change and transition the energy of this New Moon will lend itself beautifully to wishes that release you from anxiety and insecurity, inviting stability and emotional strength and resilience.

If you have been hurt in the past, this is an ideal New Moon to set wishes to invite new and harmonious relationships into your life.

If you have struggled to hold your own in relationships and have experienced an inequality in giving and receiving, this is an ideal New Moon to set wishes that request healthy, balanced, mutual intimacy in your relationships.

In your New Moon ceremonies write down your 10 wishes and open yourself to receive the guidance that you need to highlight the next steps on your pathway of manifestation. To engage with the New Moon energy at its most powerful, be sure to write your wishes down during the 8 hours following the exact time of the New Moon in your location.

- 9th July - Los Angeles 18.16
- 9th July – New York 21.16
- 10th July - London 02.16
- 10th July – Sydney 11.16
- 10th July – Auckland 13.16

My Ten New Moon Wishes

1

2

3

4

5

6

7

8

9

10

-- Wishes and Dreams --

The Full Moon in July

23rd/24th July – Full Moon in Aquarius

The Full Moon occurs when the Sun and the Moon sit directly opposite one another. It is the time in each month when the Moon has gathered light and energy from the Sun and shines at her brightest, illuminating all that needs to be seen.

Use this time each month to meditate and request illumination and guidance to support your manifestations.

It is also the very best time of the month to place your Crystals outside overnight to recharge in the powerful light of the Moon.

The Full Moon in Aquarius highlights those areas of our lives where we need to find a balance between our own self-interests and the interests of the wider collective. Balancing personal freedom with our personal responsibility to the world beyond ourselves, this Full Moon will illuminate any limiting patterns of thinking that need to be released, whilst also supporting us in finding new and innovative solutions to achieve this balance.

Each month place some rainwater or spring water in a bowl and leave it out overnight to absorb the energy of the Full Moon. Do NOT use a plastic bowl! Use glass or earthenware or any container whose fundamental ingredients come from a natural source. Collect the water afterwards and store it in a jar.

Use this Moon Water in any of your ceremonies of manifestation if you are experiencing any sort of confusion or are seeking higher guidance and an objective answer or solution.

- 23rd July - Los Angeles 19.36
- 23rd July – New York 22.36
- 24th July - London 03.36
- 24th July – Sydney 12.36
- 24th July – Auckland 14.36

-------- July 2021 --------

Journaling and Notes

Journaling and Notes

Journaling and Notes

-- July 2021 --

Journaling and Notes

Journaling and Notes

Journaling and Notes

Journaling and Notes

Journaling and Notes

--- July 2021 ---

Reflections from July

Welcome to August 2021

August 2021. A month of Conscious Activity.

In terms of manifestation this month offers much promise. The key to working with the incoming energy is to be able to see beyond our own immediate desires and follow any guidance that illuminates our unique contribution in the ever-evolving pathway to a new age.

The energetics of the New Moon in Leo on the 8th invite us to hold in mind a vision for the future and set wishes that unite the needs of the individual with those of the greater collective. In a year when so much has been systematically revealed to us, it is time to pull the information together and build a blueprint for the future. With both Venus and Mars progressing through Virgo, during the month of August we are asked not only to dream of the world that we wish to see, but also to take actions to initiate the process of manifesting this dream into reality.

For anyone who has been itching to get going and start to manifest change in real terms the energetics this month will serve you well, but be sure to look beyond your own immediate desires and align yourself with a greater vision.

Mercury, the winged messenger of the Gods, enters Virgo on the 12th, journeying to meet with the motivated fiery energy of Mars, exact on the 19th.

This collaboration invites us to enter into the kind of conversations that can transform ideas into actions. With Venus moving into Libra on the 17th adding harmony and balance to the diminishing connection between Saturn and Uranus, any changes that we initiate on the basis of universal love at this time will potentially flow into being with ease. This is a busy month that lends itself well to productivity, especially in the name of love.

The Full Moon in Aquarius on the 22nd, just 9 hours before the Sun enters Virgo, brings vibrant and flowing energy to any of the ideas that we placed into our New Moon wishing lists earlier in the month, and have subsequently taken action to put into motion.

A Full Moon will always illuminate that which we need to see in order to make adjustments, course correct, or indeed simply to validate that we are either on track... or not!

This full Moon promises an unusually flowing energetic that can potentially support us in moving something forward. With Mars and Mercury connecting favorably with Uranus, now in retrograde, we could potentially experience sudden breakthrough moments that call us to re-evaluate, indicating with clarity the next steps on our pathway of progress.

With so much potential for 'doing' this month, the Crystal that immediately came to mind to support us in our manifestations this month is Carnelian.

Carnelian has to be one of my most favorite Raw Crystals! For me, it is one of those Crystals that does exactly what is says on the tin!
The energy of Carnelian is said to restore vitality and bring motivation. Stimulating creativity, it promotes positive life choices. A powerful crystal of vibrant energy, it is said to bring courage and create a mindset that motivates for success.

If you need energy to begin a project or strength and durability to see you through to the finish line, or indeed if you are someone who struggles with a debilitating inner critic that inhibits your perseverance, then this dynamic crystal could become a great friend and ally to you.

New Moon Wishes and Intentions

8th/9th August - New Moon in Leo

This New Moon in Leo invites us to get creative! This is a magnificent energy to engage with in the creation of a brand-new vision board, encompassing all of the learning that has been brought to you during the year so far.

A New Moon in Leo naturally lends itself to wishes that focus on creativity, love and romance, playfulness, generosity and fun. The energy of a Leo New Moon also supports us in making wishes that enhance our personal passions, our leadership qualities, bring us enthusiasm and determination and encourage the building of our confidence and individual self-expression.

Given the potential to take action this month and to actually initiate our manifestations in real terms, this is a perfect new moon to make wishes that request help in building both confidence and durability. It is also perfect to set wishes that support any creative ventures that you may wish to initiate.

If you are the kind of person who procrastinates this is a perfect New Moon to wish for assistance in dispersing any resistance to your personal progress with ease.

In terms of your work life balance and your investment in relationships, love, romance and any desires you may have to bring lightheartedness and playfulness into your relationships, this New Moon is ideal for wishes that orientate in these directions.

In your New Moon ceremonies write down your 10 wishes and open yourself to receive the guidance that you need to highlight the next steps on your pathway of manifestation. To engage with the New Moon energy at its most powerful, be sure to write your wishes down during the 8 hours following the exact time of the New Moon in your location.

- 8th August - Los Angeles 06.50
- 8th August – New York 09.50
- 8th August - London 14.50
- 8th August – Sydney 23.50
- 9th August – Auckland 01.50

My Ten New Moon Wishes

1

2

3

4

5

6

7

8

9

10

The Full Moon in August

22nd/23rd August – Blue Full Moon in Aquarius

The Full Moon occurs when the Sun and the Moon sit directly opposite one another. It is the time in each month when the Moon has gathered light and energy from the Sun and shines at her brightest, illuminating all that needs to be seen.

Use this time each month to meditate and request illumination and guidance to support your manifestations.

It is also the very best time of the month to place your Crystals outside overnight to recharge in the powerful light of the Moon.

This Full Moon in Aquarius is loaded with the energetic of possibility and has the potential to bring insights and illuminations that bring clarity and direction. With so many planets in retrograde take the opportunity to meditate into a space of possibility and be open to receive the guidance needed to highlight new pathways of conscious activity to bring your visions of manifestation into form.

Each month place some rainwater or spring water in a bowl and leave it out overnight to absorb the energy of the Full Moon. Do NOT use a plastic bowl! Use glass or earthenware or any container whose fundamental ingredients come from a natural source. Collect the water afterwards and store it in a jar.

Use this Moon Water in any of your ceremonies of manifestation when you are seeking clarity of direction.

- 22nd August - Los Angeles 05.01
- 22nd August – New York 08.01
- 22nd August - London 13.01
- 22nd August – Sydney 22.01
- 23rd August – Auckland 00.01

-- August 2021 --

149

Journaling and Notes

Journaling and Notes

August 2021

Journaling and Notes

Journaling and Notes

-------- August 2021 --------

Journaling and Notes

--------------------------------- August 2021 -------------------------

Reflections from August

Welcome to September 2021

September 2021. Listen to Your Heart.

In a month when five of our major players are all in retrograde the energy invites a gentle approach, calling us to listen with our hearts rather than our minds. Continue to nurture the seeds of your wishes that were sown in August and make time for a life review.

The New Moon in Virgo on the 7th finds an exact and flowing connection with Uranus, the bringer of revolutionary ideas and thinking out of the box solutions. Use any lightbulb moments to shape your New Moon wish list and if something unusual or unexpected is revealed, listen and trust that you are being shown those things that you need to see to liberate you from past limitations.

This magical New Moon sees Venus in harmonious relationship with Jupiter, Mars in harmonious relationship with Pluto, and Mercury in harmonious relationship with Saturn.

This is an extraordinarily powerful New moon to set wishes and intentions that value our relationships, partnerships, friendships, family, home and community, and support us in achieving balance and harmony in all areas of our lives.

In a year of tough realizations, September seems to offer an opportunity to pause for breath and truly realign in ways that set a new compass for the future.

Any wishes made on this powerfully positive New Moon promises to be supported by an energy of peace and balance to initiate changes that flow into being with ease.

Hold an energetic of gratitude and appreciation as we move to the Full Moon in Pisces on the 20th.

With the messenger planet of Mercury, now preparing to move into retrograde on the 27th, squaring up to transformative Pluto, who in turn aligns favorably with the Moon, the Sun, dreamy Neptune and motivated Mars, deep conversations may reveal a truth that has needed to be heard.

As we enter the retrograde shadow period, we are asked to recognize that everything that comes to us is good information and a potential call to action.

On the 22nd September at the Equinox, the Sun moves into Libra. In the four day period around the Equinoxes and Solstices, when the Earth pauses for breath, use this time for deep meditation and open yourself to any form of healing that brings balance back into your life, both inner and outer, and make a firm commitment to any ongoing practices that will maintain and carry this balance with you into the future.

PINK CALCITE

In a month that calls for gentleness and an openness to receive, the energy of Pink Calcite reached out as our perfect Crystal companion for the month.

Calcites are without question some of the greatest healers of the Crystal family. Known as an amplifier of energy, Pink Calcite is a powerful bringer of gentleness that encourages self-love and the love of others and all of life. For me, its energy seems to radiate and embody compassion creating a deep connection that overrides the ego enabling us to relate with others Soul to Soul.

If you are fired up about something and wish to bring love into your words, thoughts and actions, then this is a magnificent crystal to carry with you. It is also said to remove fear and lessen anxiety, soothing away tension.

New Moon Wishes and Intentions

6th/7th September - New Moon in Virgo

In a month where the astro-energy naturally invites review, use the incredibly positive alignments of this New Moon in Virgo to set wishes that create balance from the inside out and that emphasize the day to day quality of your life. The energy of the New Moon in Virgo lends itself well to areas of our lives that involve our physical health and wellbeing, our careers and workplace, and our ability to be organized and efficient. It also connects to our capacity be discerning within our relationships and hold our boundaries.

Use this New Moon Energy to wish for the perfect work life balance that allows you to uphold a consistent flow of healthy energy that brings wellness in both mind, body and soul.

If you are looking to manifest a new career pathway use the energy of this New Moon to set wishes that invite a career position that aligns you with your greatest contribution.

If you are experiencing any form of dissatisfaction, conflict or challenge, particularly at work with either managers or subordinates, use this New Moon to wish for a balanced resolution that values all parties.

If you are someone who is crippled by perfectionism and carries a raging inner critic, use this New Moon to make wishes that ask to release these internal thinking patterns with ease.

In your New Moon ceremonies write down your 10 wishes and open yourself to receive the guidance that you need to highlight the next steps on your pathway of manifestation. To engage with the New Moon energy at its most powerful, be sure to write your wishes down during the 8 hours following the exact time of the New Moon in your location.

- 6th September - Los Angeles 17.51
- 6th September – New York 20.51
- 7th September - London 01.51
- 7th September – Sydney 10.51
- 7th September – Auckland 12.51

My Ten New Moon Wishes

1

2

3

4

5

6

7

8

9

10

-- Wishes and Dreams --

The Full Moon in September

20th/21st September – Full Moon in Pisces

The Full Moon occurs when the Sun and the Moon sit directly opposite one another. It is the time in each month when the Moon has gathered light and energy from the Sun and shines at her brightest, illuminating all that needs to be seen.

Use this time each month to meditate and request illumination and guidance to support your manifestations.

It is also the very best time of the month to place your Crystals outside overnight to recharge in the powerful light of the Moon.

This Full Moon in Pisces naturally beckons us to connect with a sense of greater meaning in our lives and our higher purpose. Piscean energy is often highly emotional and in terms of illuminating those aspects of our lives that need to be released this Full Moon can feel both liberating and/or a little overwhelming depending on our unique individual circumstances.

Each month place some rainwater or spring water in a bowl and leave it out overnight to absorb the energy of the Full Moon. Do NOT use a plastic bowl! Use glass or earthenware or any container whose fundamental ingredients come from a natural source. Collect the water afterwards and store it in a jar.

Use this Moon Water in any of your ceremonies when you need emotional release. It is also perfect to add a power boost in ceremonies to manifest your calling and your higher purpose.

- 20th September - Los Angeles 16.54
- 20th September – New York 19.54
- 21st September - London 00.54
- 21st September – Sydney 09.54
- 21st September – Auckland 11.54

-- September 2021 --

Journaling and Notes

Journaling and Notes

September 2021

Journaling and Notes

---------------------------- September 2021 ----------------------------

September 2021

Journaling and Notes

-------------------------------- September 2021 --------------------------------

September 2021

Journaling and Notes

Reflections from September

-- Journaling & Notes --

174

Welcome to October 2021

October 2021. Coming Together and Finding New Hope.

The first week of October invites us to continue with the deep reflective processes of September.

The New Moon in Libra on the 6th sees transformative Pluto stationing direct, and with the Sun, the Moon, motivated Mars and the messenger Mercury lining up in Libra and forming flowing connections with karmic Saturn and expansive Jupiter, this promises to be a powerful time that is particularly conducive to the setting of wishes and intentions that forge new initiatives designed to bring unity.

Wow!

Saturn stations direct on the 11th, followed by Mercury and Jupiter on the 18th.

This change in direction heralds an energetic shift that adds momentum to the development of the much needed changes that have been calling to us throughout the year and are beginning to find their feet and show the promise of new horizons.

In any major periods of accelerated growth and transformation there will inevitably be a degree of challenge as we work out how best to forge new pathways that support us in navigating to new ways of being.

Calling all Spiritual Warriors to action!

The Full Moon in Aries on the 20th, collaborating with Mars and Pluto fuels an emotional intensity that has the potential to enflame our passions and fire us up.

With Jupiter expanding the mix, be sure to channel this energy consciously into your manifestations and invest your passion in mindful, considered actions that reflect the greater whole.

With Neptune bringing a Spiritual dimension to the mix and Uranus still in retrograde, use this energetic to bring definition to your future plans, whilst simultaneously remaining grounded.

The Sun enters Scorpio on the 23rd, naturally inviting us to dive deep and as Saturn and Uranus prepare to meet with Jupiter and Pluto in early November, in your skills of manifestation, develop your ability to embrace Spiritual Empathy and practice the art of allowing.

We end this month with the festivals of Samhain in the Northern Hemisphere and Beltane in the Southern Hemisphere. At these pivotal turning points in the natural cycles of the earth, it is said that 'the veil is thin' and that the space between worlds allows an ease of communication with those who love and guide us, in particular at this time, with our ancestors.

Take time to honor both your own journey and those who have walked before you as we prepare to enter a new cycle of evolutionary growth.

With such an interesting mix of astro-energy this month, the transformational qualities of Labradorite seem to offer us exactly the balance that we need to remain reflective whilst consciously channel any highly charged emotional energy.

Labradorite is known as a Stone of Transformation and is said to bring the wearer strength and perseverance, its energy heightening Spiritual connections whilst grounding and strengthening trust in both ourselves and the Universe.

It is known as a 'revealer' in that it shows us the Truth behind the illusion and so cuts through the concepts of our limited ego mind.
I find this stone aids and enhances my creativity helping to bring focus and channel energy into conscious, direct actions of manifestation.

New Moon Wishes and Intentions

6th/7th October - New Moon in Libra

The energy of the New Moon in Libra is naturally inclined to support all aspects of balance and harmony in our lives and in our relationships. If you are seeking to make wishes that involve the realignment of any aspect of your wellbeing this is a perfect New Moon to set wishes that realign and rebalance your Chakras.

In light of the powerful astrological alignments this month, should you have any inner psychological patterns that lower your self-esteem this is a perfect new moon to request that these thinking patterns leave you and are easily let go of.

If you are seeking long term balance and harmony within relationship and desire marriage and a union of equality then the Libra new moon is the most amazing moon to set wishes in this area of your life and create a calling in love new moon ceremony.

If you are someone who struggles to negotiate effectively then this is an ideal new moon to ask for assistance in releasing any issues surrounding this and requesting the development of fluent communications that are fair and equal to all parties.

In your New Moon ceremonies write down your 10 wishes and open yourself to receive the guidance that you need to highlight the next steps on your pathway of manifestation. To engage with the New Moon energy at its most powerful, be sure to write your wishes down during the 8 hours following the exact time of the New Moon in your location.

- 6th October - Los Angeles 04.05
- 6th October – New York 07.05
- 6th October - London 12.05
- 6th October – Sydney 22.05
- 7th October – Auckland 00.05

My Ten New Moon Wishes

1

2

3

4

5

6

7

8

9

10

-- Wishes and Dreams ---

The Full Moon in October

20ᵗʰ/21ˢᵗ October – Full Moon in Aries

The Full Moon occurs when the Sun and the Moon sit directly opposite one another. It is the time in each month when the Moon has gathered light and energy from the Sun and shines at her brightest, illuminating all that needs to be seen.

Use this time each month to meditate and request illumination and guidance to support your manifestations.

It is also the very best time of the month to place your Crystals outside overnight to recharge in the powerful light of the Moon.

The Full Moon in Aries inspires us pursue our dreams with passion, illuminating those areas of our lives that are on track... as well as those that are not! The energy of an Aries Full Moon naturally lends itself to the initiation of new beginnings, bringing us the courage to step into our fullest potential, aligning our actions with true purpose and direction.

Each month place some rainwater or spring water in a bowl and leave it out overnight to absorb the energy of the Full Moon. Do NOT use a plastic bowl! Use glass or earthenware or any container whose fundamental ingredients come from a natural source. Collect the water afterwards and store it in a jar.

Use this Moon Water in any of your ceremonies that are connected to initiating new beginnings or when you need courage to either step into the new, or to hold your direction with purpose and intent.

- **20ᵗʰ October - Los Angeles 07.56**
- **20ᵗʰ October – New York 10.56**
- **21ˢᵗ October - London 15.56**
- **21ˢᵗ October – Sydney 01.56**
- **21ˢᵗ October – Auckland 03.56**

-- October 2021 --

Journaling and Notes

Journaling and Notes

--------------------- October 2021 ---------------------

Journaling and Notes

-------------------------------- October 2021 --------------------------------

October 2021

Reflections from October

Welcome to November 2021

November 2021. Release the Old... Embrace the New.

We begin November with an intense New mon in Scorpio on the 4th, making an exact squared connection with Uranus the great awakener and bringer of change, who in turn squares up to the structured and ordered energy of Saturn.

With the fiery energy of the warrior planet Mars adding to the mix, this collaboration brings a dynamic start to the month.

Throughout 2021 Saturn and Uranus have brought an energetic that not only highlights outmoded mindsets and structures that need to change, but their collaboration also demands that we take up the challenge in real terms.

Whilst this may not have been entirely comfortable, if we make the effort to stand back and view the bigger picture, particularly in the context of the birthing of humanity into a new age, then we can see that this powerful duo have brought us the influences that were needed to shock us out of our comfort zone and stretch us into new and innovative ways of approaching problems and finding solutions.

Whilst this isn't always easy or comfortable it does actually bring us real opportunity to embrace new ways of seeing and new ways of doing.

When Mars is joined by Mercury, the great communicator, exact on the 10th, the following 9 day window brings real opportunity to let go of past grievances and overcome any limitations that have previously slowed down or inhibited the arrival of solutions, that will forge new ways of being, in the creation of a more balanced and unified future.

Eclipse season brings with it the potential for us to access powerful portals of insights that span time and allow us to relinquish past patterns and step into a space of higher learning and evolutionary growth.

When we reach the Full Moon Eclipse in Taurus on the 19th, Mars, Uranus and Saturn firmly hold this energetic for change, whilst the Sun and Moon collaborate with expansive Jupiter enhancing an energetic of newfound optimism and ideas of expanded possibilities.

The Sun enters Sagittarius on the 22nd aligning favorably with the energy of Mercury, the winged messenger of the gods.

This energetic stays with us through to the end of the month offering real space for creative solutions to be found to bring into being, a unified, balanced and fulfilled vision of the future, both personally and collectively.

The Power of Collective Prayer

December will see the final squaring up of Saturn and Uranus in this year of pivotal transition and change.

Thank you so much for joining me and please spread the word.

Third Collective Prayer for 2021 December 24th – 29th inclusive.

Embracing the overall energy of November and aligning with the potential to create a unified, balanced and fulfilled vision of the future, both personally and collectively the Crystal that offered to walk alongside us this month is the powerful and energetic Sunstone.

The energy of Sunstone is passionate, vibrant energetic and full of vitality. Forming a connection between the heart and the Sun, it is said to boost our life force, alleviating stress and any fear-based energies, replacing them with positive high vibrational energy.

Not surprisingly, Sunstone is associated with good luck and good fortune. Aligning all Chakras to create a powerful energetic flow, this magical stone bypasses the limitations of the ego mind allowing out true self to shine.

This is a powerful little crystal to carry when setting intentions!

New Moon Wishes and Intentions

4th/5th November - New Moon in Scorpio

The energy of a New Moon in Scorpio naturally lends itself to wishes that embrace areas of change and personal transformation that go deep!

This is a perfect New Moon to support us in setting wishes that invite greater personal empowerment and address any issues of power dynamics within our relationships and dealings with others. Given the intensity of the dynamics this month, the timing is perfect to delve deep and request help in releasing any inner blocks that have been limiting our potential with ease.

This New Moon is an ideal time to wish for deeper emotional and sexual connections and a soul mate relationship.

The energy also supports our business partnerships and our collaborations with larger organizations.

In your New Moon ceremonies write down your 10 wishes and open yourself to receive the guidance that you need to highlight the next steps on your pathway of manifestation.

To engage with the New Moon energy at its most powerful, be sure to write your wishes down during the 8 hours following the exact time of the New Moon in your location.

- 4th November - Los Angeles 14.14
- 4th November – New York 17.14
- 4th November - London 21.14
- 5th November – Sydney 08.14
- 5th November – Auckland 10.14

My Ten New Moon Wishes

1

2

3

4

5

6

7

8

9

10

The Full Moon in November

19ᵗʰ November – Full Moon Eclipse in Taurus

The Full Moon occurs when the Sun and the Moon sit directly opposite one another. It is the time in each month when the Moon has gathered light and energy from the Sun and shines at her brightest, illuminating all that needs to be seen.

Use this time each month to meditate and request illumination and guidance to support your manifestations.

It is also the very best time of the month to place your Crystals outside overnight to recharge in the powerful light of the Moon.

The energy of a Full Moon in Taurus inspires us to push through, regardless of any obstacles in our path. When our actions are in pursuit of higher ideals, the energy flow will work with us bringing us staying power and stamina, however we must also be mindful not to act like a bull in a china shop pushing through without thought or regard and so a Taurus Full Moon will also highlight areas of our lives where we perhaps need to slow down and tread a little more lightly.

Each month place some rainwater or spring water in a bowl and leave it out overnight to absorb the energy of the Full Moon. Do NOT use a plastic bowl! Use glass or earthenware or any container whose fundamental ingredients come from a natural source. Collect the water afterwards and store it in a jar.

Use this Moon Water in any of your ceremonies where you need to find perseverance and staying power, or perhaps to slow something down to a manageable pace bringing slow and steady progress.

- 19ᵗʰ November - Los Angeles 00.57
- 19ᵗʰ November – New York 03.57
- 19ᵗʰ November - London 08.57
- 19ᵗʰ November – Sydney 19.57
- 19ᵗʰ November – Auckland 21.57

My Full Moon Insights and Illuminations

Journaling and Notes

Journaling and Notes

Journaling and Notes

Journaling and Notes

Journaling and Notes

Journaling and Notes

Journaling and Notes

-- Journaling & Notes --

Welcome to December 2021

December 2021. A New Dawn.

If there was ever a month when the universal energies lend themselves the creation of a collective vision for the future, then this is it!

December begins with a New Moon Eclipse in Sagittarius on the 4th, aligning favorably with Saturn, Father time. From the perspective of manifestation, this promises to be one of the most powerful New Moons of the year!

The connection between energetic, motivated Mars, dreamy insightful Neptune and transformational Pluto is just flowing, and this trio hold the energy for the entire month.

Add to this the dynamic portal of opportunity that is always present in eclipse season plus the influence of Uranus, heralding exciting, albeit sometimes disruptive, opportunities for change, take time to invest in your wishes and intentions and keep your dreams firmly in mind as we navigate this final month of a year of profound transition into a New Age and New Dawn.

Set your wishes at the New Moon Eclipse, open yourself to receive guidance, and hold your vision whilst simultaneously giving it room to breathe and to grow.

Venus stations direct on the 15th, and moves into retrograde, bringing our attention to those aspects of our lives that really matter. Joining Pluto for the Full Moon in Gemini on the 19th Venus in retrograde illuminates any aspects of our lives that need to come back into balance and with Jupiter bringing a powerful and favorable influence to this Full Moon, we are invited to expand our visions beyond concerns of the ego and to dream of a world that is centered in universal love.

Mercury, the winged messenger of the Gods, and Uranus, the great awakener, communicate well, bringing the potential for fruitful conversations that help in overcoming resistance to change.

The Solstice energy on the 21st, invites us to align with the Earth and as she pauses for breath, we honor and acknowledge the powerful shifts of the natural world of which we too are a part.

The Sun moves into Capricorn and we move towards the final squaring up between Uranus and Saturn, exact on Christmas Eve. Remain grounded and meditate into the incoming energy and open yourself to receive guidance.

We end December with Jupiter moving into Pisces on the 29th, bringing renewed optimism and hope to our dreams and wishes. Make a commitment to yourself to follow through with any actions that are called for in support of your manifestations and as we approach a New year and the first New Moon of 2022 on January 2nd in Capricorn, take time to reflect and plan for stability and a future that holds a reverence for the unity of all of life.

The Third Collective Prayer for 2021
December 24th – 29th inclusive.

Saturn, the planet of structure and the bearer of karmic lessons and the lighting spirit of Uranus, the great awakener square up for the final time this year and what an extraordinary time to lean into the power of collective prayer and the energetic of giving.

Merry Christmas everyone.

In the intensity of this collaboration please take a moment for a minute of silent prayer at 7pm each day during this period. Join me in holding the higher vibration of this energetic and channel the extraordinary potential of this energy into a collective vision of a united humanity, one that is attuned not only to the needs of our fellow human beings, but to all of life that surrounds us.

We end this powerful year of transformative change and opportunity by honoring the extraordinary qualities embodied by Selenite who aligns with our beautiful Moon. Selenite draws its name came from Selene, the Greek Goddess of the Moon, and just as the Moon gathers light from the Sun and redistributes it across the Earth, so too Selenite literally embodies and radiates light.

This magical and illuminating crystal can be used for healing in its own right, or used with other crystals. For me, Selenite is one of the essentials in my Crystal toolkit and a personal favorite. I keep several Selenite sticks and much as I would put my crystals out overnight to re-charge at the Full Moon, I use my selenite sticks to re-charge the energy of my other crystals.

Associated with the alignment of the third eye, crown and etheric chakras, this powerful crystal is a must for anyone seeking to connect with their Guides and Angels, also known as an Abundance Stone, perhaps a reflection of its generous and giving nature, it is said to raise our awareness and connect us with our higher self.

New Moon Wishes and Intentions

3rd/4th December – Super New Moon Eclipse in Sagittarius

The energy of the New Moon Eclipse in Sagittarius naturally embraces the qualities of renewed optimism, holding hope, overcoming depression, and the finding of solutions. This energetic also naturally enhances any wishes that connect with our personal sense of freedom, the rights and freedom of others, truth, liberty and justice.

Wishes set at this time are also perfect in bringing increased motivation, with stamina and determination to see something through.

If you have struggled with procrastination, then this is a perfect new moon to request that these thinking patterns leave you and are easily let go of.

If you are seeking spontaneity and adventure and have been searching to find your calling to align you with renewed energy, hope and inspiration, this is a perfect new moon to request signposts to show you what steps to take next to bring a clarity of direction easily and quickly.

In your New Moon ceremonies write down your 10 wishes and open yourself to receive the guidance that you need to highlight the next steps on your pathway of manifestation. To engage with the New Moon energy at its most powerful, be sure to write your wishes down during the 8 hours following the exact time of the New Moon in your location.

- 3rd December - Los Angeles 23.43
- 4th December – New York 02.43
- 4th December - London 07.43
- 4th December – Sydney 18.43
- 4th December – Auckland 20.43

My Ten New Moon Wishes

1

2

3

4

5

6

7

8

9

10

-- Wishes and Dreams --

The Full Moon in December

18th/19th December – Full Moon in Gemini

The Full Moon occurs when the Sun and the Moon sit directly opposite one another. It is the time in each month when the Moon has gathered light and energy from the Sun and shines at her brightest, illuminating all that needs to be seen.

Use this time each month to meditate and request illumination and guidance to support your manifestations.

It is also the very best time of the month to place your Crystals outside overnight to recharge in the powerful light of the Moon.

A Gemini Full Moon governs areas of our personality and development that connect to learning, reading, writing speaking, listening and all areas of communication. The Full Moon in Gemini will illuminate any aspects of our lives that can be extended, grown and developed further to enhance better and more fluent communication, whether with ourselves or with others.

Each month place some rainwater or spring water in a bowl and leave it out overnight to absorb the energy of the Full Moon. Do NOT use a plastic bowl! Use glass or earthenware or any container whose fundamental ingredients come from a natural source. Collect the water afterwards and store it in a jar.

Use this Moon Water in any of your ceremonies where fluent and easy communication is required to enhance your manifestations.

- 18th December - Los Angeles 20.35
- 18th December – New York 23.35
- 19th December - London 04.35
- 19th December – Sydney 15.35
- 19th December – Auckland 17.35

Journaling and Notes

December 2021

Journaling and Notes

-------------------------------- December 2021 --------------------------------

Journaling and Notes

Journaling and Notes

Journaling and Notes

-------------------- December 2021 --------------------

Journaling and Notes

December 2021

Reflections from December

-- Journaling & Notes --

222

-- Journaling & Notes --

The Power of Collective Prayer

Thank you so much for joining me in the one minute of silent prayer during the most pivotal and intense periods of potential challenge and change offered by the influence of Saturn and Uranus during 2021.

I hope that the information within this Journal, and also the Art of Manifestation Diary, have supported you on your own personal pathway of evolution during these unprecedented times of growth and change.

I look forward to reconnecting with you again in 2022.

Namaste

Blessings to you for the coming year of 2022

The Art of Manifestation Oracle Cards

The Art of Manifestation Oracle Cards featured in this diary are available to buy from the A-Z store at; https://www.azemotionalhealth.store/

They are also available on Amazon.

About the Author

Jenny Florence is a best-selling Author and her professional career as an Accredited BACP, UKRC Registered Counsellor spanned over 28 years working with individuals, couples and teams.

Her books include;

7 Steps to Spiritual Empathy – Learn to Listen, Change your Life! Mindfulness meets Emotional Awareness - 7 Steps to Learn the Language of your Emotions and the I Choose Love Series which includes I Choose Love – the A-Z Guidebook for the Spiritual Warrior, the Art of Manifestation Astro-Moon Diary and Journal and the Art of Manifestation Oracle Cards.

Her books are available from Amazon or from the A-Z of Emotional Health online Store.

https://www.azemotionalhealth.store/

She first began reading Tarot cards as a teenager and has also studied astrology. She posts free weekly and bi-monthly readings on her YouTube Channel which align with the natural cycles of the Moon.

She is the founder and creator of the A-Z of Emotional Health on-line Video Library, a free Public Resource, dedicated to understanding Emotional and Mental Wellness from a holistic perspective.

For more information visit her Free on-line Library;
https://www.azemotionalhealth.com/

Or follow her on Social Media;

YouTube - http://www.youtube.com/c/AZEmotionalHealth

Facebook - https://www.facebook.com/azofemotionalhealth/

Made in the USA
Columbia, SC
30 June 2021